Go FUN!

SLYLOCK FOX

MYSTERY PUZZLES

BOB WEBER, JR.
AND BOB WEBER, SR.

Andrews McMeel
Publishing®

Kansas City · Sydney · London

Andrews McMeel Publishing, LLC
an Andrews McMeel Universal company
1130 Walnut Street, Kansas City, Missouri 64106

www.andrewsmcmeel.com

Puzzles by Bob Weber, Jr. and Bob Weber, Sr.

15 16 17 18 19 PAH 10 9 8 7 6 5 4 3 2 1

ISBN: 978-1-4494-6900-9

Made by:
The P.A. Hutchison Company

Address and location of production:
400 Penn Avenue, Mayfield, PA 18433 USA

1st printing – 06/24/15

1

A witness claims she observed a bank robber race into the Forest Museum. A trail of loose money leads to the medieval room. What evidence led Slylock Fox to suspect that the robber is hiding inside the suit of armor on the far left?

2

Count Weirdly announced that superintelligent aliens, living five million light years away from Earth, have answered his intergalactic radio message. Weirdly says he asked for and received instruction on how to build a "Supreme Ruler" crown. The count claims that whoever wears the crown will control the minds and actions of all Earth creatures. How does Slylock Fox know Count Weirdly is telling an astronomical lie?

Artist Georgia Opossum says Shady Shrew
stole a bowl of fruit she was painting. Ms.
Opossum claims that when she took a phone
call from her agent, the shrew grabbed the
bowl and bolted. Shady insists he bought
this fruit four days ago. What evidence did
Slylock Fox observe that suggests Shady
Shrew is lying?

4

Slick Smitty and world-renowned paleontologist Dr. Weimaraner are fighting over an awesome dinosaur skull. They both insist they were the first to find the fossil. Why is Slylock Fox nearly certain that Slick Smitty was not the first to find the fossil?

Slylock Fox teaches a criminology course at the university. He suspects the bear cheated on today's essay exam. Instead of writing the essay in class as he was supposed to do, Slylock thinks the bear turned in an essay that was written outside of class. What evidence caused Slylock's suspicion?

The crew has abandoned this sinking cargo ship. There's one lifeboat remaining. It has enough room for Slylock Fox, Max Mouse, and just one crate. There is no time to open several crates and pack a variety of items. Considering they may be adrift for many days, which crate should Slylock select?

7

When Slylock Fox and Max Mouse entered the
bakery shop to buy a birthday cake, a thief
was stealing money from the manager's office
safe. The robber's accomplice watched at the
counter to make sure the clerk did not say
anything to Slylock. How did she alert him that
a robbery was in progress?

8

Angry citizens reported prank calls coming from Cassandra Cat's landline phone earlier this evening. The feline insists she just arrived home a few minutes ago, lit scented candles, and started water for a bubble bath. Why does Slylock Fox doubt Cassandra's story?

In order to rescue Slylock Fox, Max Mouse must get the rope across the gorge. But the poor mouse can't throw the heavy rope that far. What instructions could Slylock give his little buddy that would result in the fox getting hold of the rope and eventually crossing?

Slylock Fox needs to get a secret handwritten and signed document to Chief Mutt's home within the hour. But Slylock is being followed, and he doesn't want the one tailing him to see where the document is going. How could Slylock Fox solve this problem?

11

Count Weirdly is racing to Slylock Fox's house to bust in and eliminate incriminating evidence on Slylock's computer. If Weirdly and Slylock travel at the same average speed, why will Slylock arrive at his house ten minutes before the count?

One of these suspects stole an ancient
Egyptian sculpture from the Forest Museum.
Slylock Fox is holding a box that contains
physical evidence dropped by the thief at the
crime scene. What do you think is in the box,
and which suspect do you believe is guilty?

A burglar wearing a mask tied up Sir Hound and stole money and valuables from his mansion. Before the intruder fled the crime scene, he used a cloth and bottle of spray cleaner to wipe away his fingerprints. But Slylock Fox discovered the burglar's fingerprints on one item in this room. Which item was it?

14

Moments ago, one of these two workers
stole a secret design file from the Mega
Toy Company. Then the thief unscrewed
an air duct wall panel, hid the file inside,
and replaced the panel. Which worker does
Slylock Fox suspect is guilty, and why?

Slick Smitty was supposed to bring a bowl of punch to the block party, but the bowl is empty. Smitty insists he didn't neglect his responsibility. Instead, he claims Earl Elephant slipped his trunk into the bowl and didn't take it out until he had swallowed every drop of punch. How does Slylock Fox know Slick Smitty is lying?

16

Brody Beagle claims someone stole his wristwatch while he was sleeping on his beach blanket. After carefully surveying the surrounding crime area, Slylock Fox found a suspect. Who is it?

Slylock Fox asked Max Mouse to devise a system of secret hand signals. Several hours later, Slylock asked Max if he had finished devising the signals. Max responded by tugging his right ear. What additional question could Slylock ask to find out whether that was a yes or no answer?

18

Slylock Fox suspects this large, famous painting is a fake. He believes art forger Koppy Kat stole the valuable original and replaced it with a copy. The felonious feline always leaves a visual error in his forgeries. What error did Slylock observe in the painting?

Four forest animals have had their fur and feathers burned in the past hour. The singed citizens claim Count Weirdly zapped them with a laser from his castle roof. The count insists he's innocent and says he has just returned from a ninety-minute jog. How did Slylock Fox disprove Count Weirdly's alibi?

An escaped prisoner removed a manhole cover and climbed down into the storm drainage pipes. He waded though the drainpipes until he reached the river. How can Slylock Fox quickly navigate his way through the maze of pipes to the river without a map?

21

Slylock Fox and Max Mouse sneaked into the back of a stolen truck that bank bandits used to escape. The bandits aren't talking, but Slylock soon heard something from the cabin that suggested they had just driven into a tunnel. What did Slylock hear?

Witnesses claim Harry Ape and his crew robbed a jewelry store at 1:35 p.m. today. But Harry insists he and his buddies were changing a flat tire on his car at that time. Slylock Fox asked the ape and his companions a question, then instructed them to whisper their answers in his ear. What did Slylock ask them, and how did their answers help determine Harry Ape lied?

Someone broke into Slylock Fox's office while
he and Max Mouse were away on a case. The
intruder was looking for a particular folder.
As Slylock studied the scene, he observed
evidence that suggests the folder was
removed from the top drawer. How did he
reach that conclusion?

Shady Shrew called his insurance company to report a boating accident. He claimed his boat sank after a large floating log poked a hole in one side. What evidence has convinced Slylock Fox that Shady Shrew is lying?

25

Someone stole gold coins from a museum near the park. No one saw the thief take the coins, so there isn't a description of the robber. Slylock Fox suspects one of the animals in the park is the thief. Which one?

SLYLOCK FOX
MYSTERY PUZZLES

Shady Shrew boasts he will win the Lake Loon rowboat race. He claims his custom-built telescopic glasses will allow him to focus on the finish line for the entire race. Shady says this will give him a psychological advantage over the other contestants. What does Slylock Fox think?

Mr. and Mrs. Beaver told Slylock Fox that a busy burglar entered every unlocked first-floor apartment window in this building except for theirs last night. How did the fact that the Beavers painted their apartment yesterday prevent them from being robbed?

After Karen Kangaroo's physical examination, the doctor left the room for an emergency phone call. When she returned to the exam room, she noticed that a silver bookend was missing. Karen insisted she didn't steal it. How was Slylock Fox able to gather evidence that suggested the kangaroo was hiding the bookend in her pouch without searching her?

Count Weirdly tricked Slylock Fox and Max
Mouse into entering his castle's storage closet
and then locked them in. There is a window,
but the ground is eighty feet below. How did
Slylock and Max manage to safely escape with
the forty-foot rope stored in the closet?

Ellen Elephant says a bag of peanuts was stolen from her porch just five minutes ago. She is convinced Shady Shrew is the nut-nabber. But Shady claims he bought these peanuts and has been sitting here eating them for twenty minutes. Why does Slylock Fox think Shady Shrew is lying?

The museum guard reports that while he was making his nightly rounds, he observed a statue about to be lifted toward a hole in the ceiling. The guard claims the thief dropped the rope when he saw him. Unfortunately, the guard says, many exhibit items were stolen before he arrived. Slylock Fox says the guard's story conflicts with the evidence at the scene. Why?

Slylock Fox discovered a secret underground hideout used by criminals to hide from the law. After a quick study of an empty milk carton, Slylock determined that the hideout has been occupied recently. What evidence did Slylock see that supports his conclusion?

33

The in-store detective says Reeky Rat tried to walk out of the department store wearing clothes he didn't pay for. The rat claims the clothes are his and that he entered the store just moments ago to buy a tie. Slylock Fox believes the guard. Why?

Shady Shrew accused Pelican Pete of trying to steal his boat. Shady says he had been rowing all morning, then came back, left his oars on the pier, and had lunch. He claims that when he returned his oars were gone and the pelican was in his boat. But Pete insists the boat is his and claims its motor is in the repair shop. Whom does Slylock Fox believe?

Slylock Fox is investigating a bank robbery. A pair of pigs report they heard an explosion, then saw a furry felon grab money and flee the bank. The pigs shouted, "Stop, thief!" but the startled robber merely muttered through her bill, laid an egg, and ran off. What kind of animal robbed the bank?

A rabbit claiming to be a pest control contractor gave Slylock Fox a free home inspection. He said that he killed some ants during the inspection and advises Slylock to pay him $150 to spray the entire house. But Slylock suspects the rabbit is trying to pull a scam. He doesn't believe these are real ants, but rather are poorly designed replicas. What led Slylock to that conclusion?

While Granny Squirrel took a nap, a
disrespectful, mean creep unloaded his
bags of garbage on Granny's front lawn.
Fortunately, Slylock Fox found evidence that
helped identify the dirty dumper. What did
Slylock find?

Slylock Fox and Max Mouse are stranded on a small, remote island. Rescuers are on the way, but a severe storm with huge waves is expected to arrive first. What materials from the island could Slylock use to quickly construct a flotation device?

Carla Cat says Slick Smitty stole her ring
when she dozed off in the waiting room.
Smitty insists he's innocent and complains that
Carla scared his pet homing pigeon away.
Slylock Fox searched Slick Smitty and the
room. Even though he was not able to find
the ring, Slylock is not convinced Smitty is
innocent. Why?

40

Slylock Fox and Max Mouse are trapped inside Count Weirdly's experimental hologram chamber. What three mistakes did the careless count program into this scene?

One of these suspects broke into Slylock Fox's home a short while ago. The intruder stole case files from the scarlet sleuth's office. As the thief fled, she left a piece of evidence. What do you suspect is the evidence, and who do you think is guilty?

42

Harry Ape robbed a bank yesterday and has been hiding in the bitter cold forest ever since. Max Mouse found Harry's clothes near a hole in the pond ice. After inspecting the clothes, Slylock Fox concluded that Harry Ape is nearby. What evidence did Slylock observe?

Slylock Fox posed the following problem to his detective class students: "If I have three rubber balls and one weighs slightly more than the others, how can I determine which one is heaviest in just one weighing?" How would you answer this problem?

44

Slylock Fox, Max Mouse, and Deputy Duck
tracked a robber to a secret cave once used
by pirates. As the tracking trio was closing
in on the crook, he fled through one of three
tunnels inside the cave. Slylock Fox suggests
they split up. How did he provide light for each
to explore a different tunnel?

SLYLOCK FOX

MYSTERY PUZZLES

Slylock Fox and Max Mouse are searching for
an escaped prisoner. Slylock found the core
of an apple he believes was eaten by the
prisoner. The fruit's appearance suggests he
ate it recently and may still be nearby. Why
did Slylock conclude the apple was eaten
recently?

Count Weirdly claims he loaded his 3-D bio printer with the combined genetic codes of a pig, bat, skunk, and python to create a chubby, flying, stinking, venomous creature. Though the twisted count has seemingly managed to produce a perverse pet, Slylock knows Weirdly's claim is flawed. What is wrong?

47

Slylock Fox and Max Mouse are transporting ancient artifacts to an Egyptian museum. Slylock received an alarming report that a severe windstorm is heading toward them. What action can Slylock take to reduce risk to their safety and prevent the artifacts from being damaged or blown away?

Slylock Fox and Max Mouse went to an apartment building on this freezing cold evening to investigate a burglary. A tenant told them the burglar ran into the furnace room. When Slylock and Max rushed in, the tenant locked the door. Slylock realized they had been tricked by the burglar. If the room is isolated in the building basement and no one can hear their cries for help, how could Slylock get someone's attention?

Slick Smitty entered the annual forest marathon race with helium balloons tied to his body. He says the balloons will lighten his weight, so he will be able to run faster. As race official, Slylock Fox allowed Smitty to run with the balloons. Is Slylock giving Slick Smitty an unfair advantage?

MY DREAM

Max Mouse presented the following brainteaser to his friends: "A beaver working at a construction site boasted he could outdo his 400-pound gorilla coworker. The beaver said he could haul something in a wheelbarrow over to the dump truck that the gorilla wouldn't be able to wheel back. How is that possible?" Slylock Fox knows the answer; do you?

One of these suspects stole diamond jewelry from the Forest Museum. The thief switched off the museum lights and eluded guards through the rooms and twisting halls in complete darkness. All of these criminals are night creatures, but which one does Slylock Fox believe is the most capable of this kind of escape?

Chief Mutt is threatening to issue Shady Shrew a ticket for deliberately dumping stinky garbage onto the road. But Shady insists he accidentally spilled the garbage when his truck came to a sudden stop at the traffic light. Why doesn't Slylock Fox believe Shady Shrew's excuse?

Art forger Koppy Kat stole and reproduced a painting titled *View From the Moon* from the Forest Museum. Slylock Fox is going to report Koppy to the police and return the museum's property. Given the fact that Koppy Kat always includes a visual error in his forgeries, which painting will Slylock Fox be returning?

Slylock Fox and Max Mouse are searching
for troublemaker Count Weirdly. Max sees a
glass of ice water and concludes that Weirdly
must not have been gone too long. But Slylock
Fox says Max's conclusion is based on false
evidence. What did Slylock notice that caused
him to disagree with his assistant?

Patty Panda's car was found six months after it was stolen. Patty is completely puzzled. She can't imagine how her car ended up on an island in the middle of a large lake. Slylock Fox believes he has an answer. What is Slylock's explanation?

Slylock Fox and Max Mouse entered a spectacular tomb inside an ancient Egyptian pyramid. It quickly became apparent to Slylock that someone else was here recently and may still be in the area. What piece of evidence did Slylock observe that supports his conclusion?

Slylock Fox and Max Mouse have lost their
way in a cave. One of the two tunnels ahead
leads to the surface; the other is a long and
winding dead end. How can a lit match help
Slylock determine which tunnel will lead them
to the surface?

Slick Smitty was hired by an armored truck company. On his first day on the job, Smitty claims a robber pelted him with eggs from a carton and snatched the sack of money he was carrying to the truck. Slylock Fox studied the crime scene and determined that the lack of certain evidence suggests Slick Smitty is lying. What is missing?

Slylock Fox captured Count Weirdly's creepy creature. Slylock suspects Weirdly deliberately released the mini monster into the forest to frighten citizens. The count insists an intruder sneaked up behind him while he was writing a letter and knocked him out. He says the intruder must have released the monster. Why doesn't Slylock believe him?

Construction workers unearthed a box of gold coins. Slick Smitty says he buried the box when he was seven years old. He claims the coins were a gift from his grandfather. Smitty explained how he marked the spot by driving a nail into the tree and that the nail is higher now because the tree is taller. How does Slylock Fox know Slick Smitty is lying?

One of these bears just ran five blocks from the supermarket with a stolen bottle of root beer. The other bear paid for his root beer and has been sitting at the bus stop for the past thirty minutes. How can Slylock Fox determine which of these similar-looking bears is the shoplifter?

Slylock Fox was searching for an escaped prisoner. As he paused to study a map of the area, the jailbird silently sneaked up behind him and was just about to strike the fox with a branch when Slylock quickly grabbed him. If the fox was facing the opposite direction, how did he know the bird was approaching?

Slylock Fox is at the First Forest Bank investigating a robbery. Chief Mutt and Deputy Duck believe the theft is the work of a lone robber because they say they found only one pair of gloves at the scene. But Slylock Fox observed a detail that suggests there may have been another robber. What did Slylock observe?

Count Weirdly used growth hormones to create Mike the Monster Mosquito. The beastly bug has radio receivers implanted under his exoskeleton so that Weirdly can control his every move. The twisted count is threatening to unleash the blood-sucking mutant on the forest population. Why is Slylock Fox not very alarmed?

Cassandra Cat broke into a fine jewelry manufacturer, cracked the safe, stole a tiny vial of diamonds, and hid it somewhere in her home. Where did Slylock Fox find the hidden vial of diamonds?

Slylock Fox believes the undersea painting being auctioned is a fake. He suspects art forger Koppy Kat stole the original painting created by a world-renowned nature artist, and replaced it with a copy. As usual, Koppy Kat included a visual error in his forgery. What error did Slylock find?

Tools were stolen before the construction crew arrived at the building site this morning. Max Mouse found footprints and a tire track, leading him to believe there were two thieves—one walking and the other riding a bike. Even though Slylock Fox believes both tracks are related to the robbery, he suspects there was only one thief. Why?

68

Shady Shrew is under arrest for missing his scheduled criminal court hearing today. Shady insists he overslept and didn't intentionally skip his court hearing. He claims his alarm clock failed to ring because the utility company shut off his electric power. Why does Slylock Fox think Shady Shrew's excuse is a lie?

Count Weirdly grew a genetically engineered monster maple tree in his castle laboratory. The twisted count sent the menacing maple out to hide among the normal forest maple trees. The mutant traveled too quickly for Slylock Fox and Max Mouse to follow, but Slylock knows the tree will have a difficult time hiding, even if it closes its mouth and eyes. Why?

Rachel Rabbit claims Reeky Rat and his punk bandmates are responsible for her missing garden vegetables. Reeky Rat insists they didn't carry a single vegetable away from her garden and would all be willing to make that statement for a lie-detector machine. But Slylock Fox knows that even if Reeky Rat's statement is true, the band could still be responsible for the missing vegetables. How?

Mrs. Chicken's little chick Chester fell into a fence-post hole at the beach! Chester is standing at the bottom of the three-foot-deep hole, just out of reach. What does Slylock Fox suggest be done to rescue the little peeper?

Slick Smitty says that while he was busy taking a quick shower, the chimney sweep he hired stole cash from an envelope Smitty left resting on the coffee table. Slylock Fox says evidence strongly suggests Smitty is wrong. What did Slylock observe that led him to believe the chimney sweep is innocent?

For the past twenty miles, Slylock Fox has
been closely followed by a mysterious
motorist. Max Mouse observed and reported
the driver's license plate, **OMH8**, to the police,
but the police vehicle registration files do not
contain a record of the plate. Slylock knows
why. Do you?

In the middle of the night, Walter Weasel made a daring prison escape through this hole under the courtyard fence. What evidence did Slylock Fox see that convinced him Walter had an accomplice from the outside?

Slylock Fox suspects Count Weirdly is the would-be burglar that tried to enter an open window at the Science Stuff store earlier tonight. A security guard thwarted the intruder by slamming the window down on the thief's hand. The count insists he was nowhere near the Science Stuff store and claims his hand was injured by hitting it with a hammer while building a birdhouse. Why does Slylock think Count Weirdly is lying?

Witnesses claim Harry Ape snatched the world's largest pearl from the Forest Museum then ran into the park. The big ape insists he is innocent and even offered to be searched. But Slylock Fox sees evidence that suggests the gorilla may have hidden the giant pearl in the park. Slylock thinks he knows where it is. Do you?

Max Mouse raced over to tell Slylock Fox that unusual thefts are occurring around town. A shoe, earring, glove, stereo speaker, crutch, ski, and bookend were stolen. Max is afraid his skateboard will be stolen next. Slylock Fox assured Max that an apparent pattern in the thefts suggests his skateboard will not likely be targeted. What is the pattern?

Earlier today, a reliable informant told Slylock Fox that this restaurant was going to be robbed at 5:00 p.m. Just before the robbery time arrived, someone called to tell the fox that a restaurant across town was currently being robbed and that his assistance was needed immediately. Why does Slylock suspect the call was made from inside this restaurant by the robber in an attempt to get him to leave?

Slylock Fox received complaints from angry boaters claiming Count Weirdly was splashing them with his Super-Duper Jet Ski on the lake today. Weirdly insists he wasn't at the lake. He claims he is returning from a fun day of ocean wave jumping. How did Slylock Fox detect that Count Weirdly may be lying?

The beaver reported to Slylock Fox that Slick Smitty stole his carry-on luggage while deplaning a New York to Los Angeles flight. Smitty insists the luggage is his and claims he just arrived on a flight from Hawaii. Something Smitty is wearing suggests he may not be telling the truth. What is it?

81

Lady Lynx accidentally dropped her diamond ring through a crevice in the jetty. The ring is resting on a dry rock, but it is just out of arm's reach. Which objects in this scene could help Slylock Fox retrieve the ring before the tide rises and washes it away?

Mrs. Gator says someone stole the pizza,
minus one slice she had eaten, from her
picnic table while she retrieved her son from
the playground. Slylock Fox suspects Shady
Shrew took the pizza, but the shrew insists he
bought it. Shady claims that he and his buddy
shared the pizza equally and says that Mrs.
Gator is welcome to eat the remaining slice.
Why does Slylock think Shady Shrew is lying?

Slylock Fox and Max Mouse are nearing Count Weirdly's underwater hideout. The count was alerted to their presence by his robotic sea creature, equipped with surveillance camera eyes. But Weirdly's talent for building robots is not equalled by his knowledge of marine life. Which creature is the robot?

When a support beam gave way, a boulder crashed on top of Slylock Fox's map. He needs the map to exit this cave. Slylock and Max pushed and pulled, but they couldn't get the boulder to budge. Suddenly, Slylock thought of a better way to move the boulder. What was it?

One of these two suspects stole this car from a mall parking lot and recklessly crashed it into the tree. Carefully study the accident scene for evidence with Slylock Fox. Which suspect is more likely the car thief?

Seconds ago, a pickpocket snatched a wallet
and dashed into this dance club. The victim
says Cassandra Cat is the thief. But Cassandra
insists she's innocent and claims she's been
in the club all evening. What evidence was
Slylock Fox able to obtain from the cat's
earrings that suggests she is lying?

87

Buford Bear snatched a gold necklace from Rachel Rabbit. A witness saw the robber run into the park. The officers caught him but were unable to find the necklace. Fortunately, Slylock Fox was more successful. Where did Slylock find Rachel Rabbit's gold necklace?

Count Weirdly is designing a new castle for his creepy critters and twisted experiments. The structure will be located in a distant city. The count says the answer to the following riddle will reveal the location: "The name of the city can be spelled by rearranging the letters of the word that means the opposite of less." Slylock Fox knows the city; do you?

Town park workers have laced ropes under
a heavy sculpture to gently lower it onto
a pedestal. But the foreman is wondering
how he will get the rope out from under the
flat base once it has been lowered onto the
pedestal. What does Slylock Fox suggest?

Someone broke into Slylock Fox's ski lodge
room several hours ago and stole his lift
ticket. A witness reports seeing Cassandra
Cat running from Slylock's room earlier today.
Cassandra insists she is not the thief and
claims she twisted her ankle on the slopes this
morning and was in her room icing the injured
ankle when the theft occurred. Why doesn't
Slylock Fox believe Cassandra Cat's alibi?

Harry Ape is suspected of robbing a coin and hobby shop, sandwich shop, and shoe repair shop. An informant told police that Harry Ape looted the shops on his way home from the Forest Gym. But when the big ape stated: "I didn't walk past those shops," the lie detector indicated he was telling the truth. Why is Slylock Fox not convinced Harry is innocent?

Slick Smitty stole and buried a sack of silver coins. Max Mouse found Smitty's map with directions to the hidden silver's location. But even though Max made every turn indicated and walked off the correct number of paces, he did not find the buried silver. What is Slylock Fox's explanation for Max's inability to find the silver coins?

Count Weirdly is asking rich investors for money to build an observatory atop a Las Vegas casino. Weirdly says tourists will flock to the attraction to stargaze, and he and the lucky investors will make a bundle of money. Slylock Fox says investing in Count Weirdly's project is a poor gamble. Why?

Rachel Rabbit and her daughter were on their way to buy groceries at the market when a strong gust of wind blew a fifty-dollar bill out of Rachel's hand and over to Slylock Fox's side of the ravine. How could Slylock Fox quickly and safely return the money?

Someone called police to report seeing Shady
Shrew push his car into the lake. Shady insists
he accidentally drove the car into the water
and was lucky to escape with his life as the
vehicle sank. Slylock Fox thinks Shady is
lying and suspects he submerged the car for
insurance money. What evidence supports
Slylock's suspicion?

Sir Hound says Shady Shrew stole very
valuable solid gold coins from his mansion
safe late last night. Shady insists he is
innocent and claims he was home in bed
early last night so he would be well rested for
today's fishing tournament. He says he's glad
he slept all night because the rest helped him
catch the heaviest fish and win a trophy. What
evidence did Slylock Fox observe at the pier
that makes him doubt Shady Shrew's alibi?

Ten minutes ago, someone beamed a digital signal into Benny Beaver's TV set. Now every channel defaults to the Chess Network. Slylock Fox suspects that Count Weirdly is behind the TV tampering. But Weirdly insists he's been busy eating a bowl of beef broth for the past 15 minutes. Why does Slylock Fox suspect the count is lying?

While Slylock Fox and Max Mouse spend a relaxing day at the beach with friends, Max challenges Slylock with the following riddle: "How can I throw an ordinary rubber ball as far as possible and have it return to my hand all by itself?" Slylock Fox knows the answer. Do you?

An intruder entered Slylock Fox's home in the middle of the night. The house was completely dark except for a tiny point of red light from Slylock's DVD player. The red light was not nearly bright enough to illuminate the intruder, but it did make it possible for Slylock to grab him. How?

Slylock Fox and Max Mouse observed a
fisherman calling for help as his rowboat was
sinking. The man shouted that he couldn't
swim and that his life jacket had fallen
overboard and drifted away. Slylock's first
thought was to open his trunk. What's in the
car trunk that will help save the fisherman?

SLYLOCK FOX
MYSTERY PUZZLES

101

Slylock Fox claims this famous seascape painting is the work of notorious art forger Koppy Kat. Slylock informed the auctioneer of the feline's favorite habit of including a visual error in each of his forgeries. Where is the error in this painting?

Someone stole money from the beach snack shop about two minutes ago. Everyone in this scene insists they are innocent, and all claim they haven't visited the snack shack for at least thirty minutes. Slylock knows one of them is lying. Which one?

103

Mean-spirited e-mail messages were sent from Ms. Rabbit's work computer to coworkers. She strongly denies writing or sending the e-mails and says someone may have sneaked onto her computer while she was away from her office and guessed her e-mail password or hacked her computer. Why does Slylock Fox lean toward believing Ms. Rabbit is innocent?

104

Becky Beaver says Count Weirdly used his laser machine to zap and fry her prized flower garden ten minutes ago. Weirdly insists he is innocent. The count says he was asleep in the tub for the last hour and only woke up when they knocked on the bathroom door. Why does Slylock Fox think Count Weirdly is lying?

105

Grandpa Goat claims Slick Smitty stole apples and oranges from a gift basket in his hospital room. Smitty says he never entered Grandpa's room. But Slylock Fox says Smitty is lying because his prints were found in Grandpa's room around the area of the basket. How is that possible, considering Slick Smitty's fingers are securely bandaged?

The night watchman claims a robber sneaked up behind him and bound, gagged, and blindfolded him. He says the thief then drove a green truck onto the construction site and loaded it with valuable tools and supplies before speeding away. Slylock Fox suspects the guard is lying and may be the robber's accomplice. Why?

Someone stole a very valuable antique chess set with solid gold chessman from Sir Hound's mansion early this morning. An informant claims Slick Smitty is the thief and that he is hiding on this tiny island. Smitty insists he couldn't be the thief because he's been marooned on this island for the past five days. What is it about Slick Smitty's appearance that led Slylock Fox to doubt his alibi?

Moments ago, Slylock Fox witnessed Roger Raccoon stealing Mrs. Beaver's gold wedding ring. The raccoon dropped the ring as Slylock chased the cowardly crook. Where is Mrs. Beaver's ring now?

MYSTERY PUZZLES

109

Slylock Fox believes Count Weirdly is working on a diabolical plan that includes building a giant, indestructible attack robot. Slylock convinced the Forest Security Agency to place a listening and video device shaped like a ball in Weirdly's project planning and design room. Unfortunately, the spy device recently started transmitting all black images and muffled sound. Why?

Harry Ape is suspected of robbing a bank this afternoon. But Harry insists he is innocent and claims he and his mother have been at this campground site since early this morning. He says he never saw the $15,000 of stolen bank cash that Max Mouse found hidden near their campsite. Why does Slylock Fox think Harry Ape is lying?

Chief Mutt pulled Cassandra Cat over for speeding. Cassandra said she has never received a speeding violation and hasn't exceeded the speed limit since leaving the Forest Fashion Mall exactly fifteen minutes ago. Slylock Fox doesn't know the validity of Cassandra's statement regarding her past driving record, but he's convinced she's fibbing about her road speed today. Why?

A restaurant diner ordered and ate four
courses of the most expensive dishes on
the menu before jumping up from his table,
dashing into the kitchen, and sprinting out a
rear exit without paying his bill. The chef and
his assistant were coming out of the walk-in
refrigerator when the diner ran past them.
Despite coming face to face with the criminal,
both told Slylock Fox they could not give a
description. How is that possible?

Poor Chief Mutt can't do police work this morning because he found his uniform destroyed. The cackling Count Weirdly says a swarm of hungry moths must have invaded the chief's closet overnight and feasted on the uniform. Why does Slylock Fox suspect Count Weirdly actually did the damage and planted the moths as a decoy?

During a weenie roast, Reeky Rat posed the following challenge to his punk pals: *"For ten bucks, I will do 1,000 push-ups."* Slylock Fox knows that if anyone makes that deal with the rat exactly as stated he runs great risk of being swindled. Why?

115

Count Weirdly built a robot to frighten local citizens. The robot's glowing eyes send a live video feed to Weirdly's castle monitor, enabling him to guide the roaming robot's actions. What can Slylock Fox do to impair Count Weirdly's ability to control the rampaging robot?

A painting by a world-renowned nature artist was stolen from the Forest Museum last week. The missing masterpiece is now in Koppy Kat's art studio. The feline forger has already painted a copy of the artwork. As usual, Koppy's version features a visual error. Which one does Slylock Fox suspect is the original painting?

Solutions

1   One of the loose bills is under the foot. The money would be lying on top if the suit of armor had not been moved since the bank robber entered the room.

2   Radio waves travel through space at the speed of light. It would take five million years for Count Weirdly's message to reach the aliens and another five million years to receive the answer.

3   There are green bananas in the fruit bowl. If they were purchased four days ago, they probably would have turned yellow by now.

4   Slylock Fox noticed Slick Smitty's footprints overlapping Dr. Weimaraner's footprints. This evidence suggests that Smitty arrived after Weimaraner.

5   The bear turned in a paper with three holes. That paper doesn't match the paper in the four-ring binder he brought to class.

6   Slylock should select the coconuts. They are a food source, but more importantly they contain coconut milk, which supplies water they will need to survive.

7   Instead of writing "Happy Birthday" on the cake, the clever counter clerk wrote the word "robbers."

8   Slylock observed a significant amount of liquid wax spill when Max Mouse accidently knocked over the candle. There wouldn't be that much melted wax if Cassandra had lit the candle a few minutes ago.

9   Slylock could tell Max to cast his fishing line across the gorge, then remove the remaining line from the pole and tie it securely to the end of the rope. Slylock could use the fishing line to pull the rope over to his side of the gorge, then tie the rope to the bridge post, and escape by crossing with his hands on the rope.

10 Slylock ordered pizza to be delivered to Chief Mutt's home and sneaked the secret signed document inside the pizza box.

11 Count Weirdly is driving on a winding road, while Slylock Fox can fly with his jetpack on a nearly straight, direct route. Slylock will arrive at his house ten minutes sooner than Weirdly because he will travel less distance.

12 One of the raccoon's coat buttons has been replaced by a safety pin. The box contains his missing button. Slylock suspects the raccoon is the thief.

13 The burglar absentmindedly left fingerprints on the bottle of cleaner he used to wipe away the prints.

14 The anteater's Phillips-head screwdriver does not match the screws in the wall panel. The stork's screwdriver does fit the screws. Slylock suspects the bird is guilty.

15 Earl couldn't have swallowed the punch with his trunk because elephants can't drink through their trunks. They suck liquid into their trunks and then squirt it into their mouths.

16 Slylock suspects the snack shack employee stole the wristwatch. Notice he is wearing a watch on both arms.

17 Slylock could tug his right ear and ask "Did you do this?" Whatever Max did in reply it would mean yes.

18 The salmon in the painting are swimming downstream, but when salmon leave the ocean and travel in streams to reproduce, they swim upstream. Generally, the adult salmon die after spawning and only the babies swim back downstream to the ocean.

19 Slylock Fox checked Count Weirdly's pulse rate and discovered it was not consistent with a person who had just jogged 90 minutes. The count is guilty.

20 If Slylock follows the water's flow direction in the pipes, it will eventually lead him to the river.

21 Slylock heard the music from the cabin radio suddenly turn to static. Being inside the tunnel blocked the truck's radio reception. When they exited the tunnel, Slylock called Chief Mutt and gave him vital location information.

22 Slylock Fox asked them which tire on the car was flat. They each whispered a different answer. Slylock called Chief Mutt, and soon bags of bank money were discovered in the car's trunk.

23 The thief opened the bottom drawer first so he wouldn't have to close each drawer to examine the next one. He didn't find the folder until he had reached the top drawer.

24 The splintered wood around the hole points outward. The hole was made from inside the boat. Slylock Fox suspects Shady Shrew intentionally sank the boat to fraudulently collect insurance money.

25 The raccoon on the seesaw couldn't hold the heavier bear off the ground unless he was carrying something heavy. Since gold is one of the heaviest metals, Slylock suspects the raccoon is the thief and has hidden the coins in his clothes.

26 Even if it were true that focusing on the finish line improved performance, Slylock Fox knows it wouldn't matter. Rowing is performed by facing backward to the direction of travel. Shady Shrew would be staring at the starting line!

27 The beavers are sloppy painters. Slylock Fox noticed their apartment window is sealed shut with gobs of dried paint.

28 Patients are routinely weighed during physical examinations. Slyock Fox weighed the kangaroo again and discovered she had suddenly gained ten pounds.

29 Slylock unwound the rope to form two thinner forty-foot-long sections. Then he tied the sections together to form an eighty-foot rope.

30 If Shady Shrew had been eating peanuts in this spot for twenty minutes, there would be empty peanut shells. No peanut shells were found on the ground or in the bag.

31 If the rope was dropped as it was about to be used to lift the statue, it would not be under the statue. The guard fabricated the story to cover himself because he is the thief.

32 The expiration date on the milk container has not yet passed.

33 It is raining outside. Reeky Rat's clothes are dry and he has no umbrella. If he had just entered the store moments ago, his clothes and everything exposed would be wet.

34 Slylock Fox believes Pete. The boat doesn't have any oarlocks. Shady Shrew couldn't have been rowing the boat all morning.

35 According to the pair of pigs, the thief has fur, a bill, and laid an egg. Slylock Fox is certain the bank robber is a platypus.

36 Ants are insects, and all insects have six legs. None of the ants the rabbit presented have six legs. Further inspection revealed they are plastic.

37 Slylock Fox found an opened postal envelope with the dumper's name and address in the garbage mess.

38 Coconuts float. Slylock Fox could wrap and tie the beached fishing net around a collection of coconuts.

39 Slylock Fox knows that the pigeon will instinctively fly home. He suspects Slick Smitty attached the ring to the bird's leg. A trip to Smitty's house proves Slylock correct.

40 The floating anchor, webbed feet on the owl, and a star inside the crescent moon.

41 The evidence bag contains a heel that matches the heel-less shoe that Cassandra Cat is wearing. The felonious feline is the case file thief.

42 Slylock Fox believes Harry Ape fell through the ice, and after climbing out of the water, took off his wet clothes due to the frigid temperatures. The sleuth suspects the ape is nearby because the wet clothes are not yet frozen.

SOLUTIONS

43 Put one ball on each side of the balance scale and leave the remaining ball off. If the scale tips, it will be obvious which ball is heaviest. But if they balance, you'll know the ball not on the scale is the heaviest.

44 Slylock Fox used the old pirate sword to slice the candle, giving each a third to light his way.

45 The flesh of the apple core is still white. The flesh of an apple soon turns brown when chemicals in the fruit react with oxygen in the air.

46 The python is not a venomous snake. It kills its prey by suffocation. Count Weirdly's creature is not venomous.

47 Slylock and Max can bury the artifacts, and then dig a hole to shelter themselves until the windstorm passes.

48 Slylock Fox can shut off the furnace. Since it is a freezing cold evening, it won't be long before the building gets very chilly. Someone will soon come to check the furnace.

49 Slylock Fox is not giving Slick Smitty an unfair advantage. The balloons will add air resistance and actually slow Slick Smitty down.

50 The beaver can haul the gorilla in a wheelbarrow over to the dump truck. The gorilla will not be able to haul himself back in a wheelbarrow.

51 The bat is most capable of pulling off an escape in total darkness. This flying mammal can rely on a radar-like system of ultrasonic sound waves to avoid obstacles in complete darkness.

52 If Shady Shrew made a sudden stop at the traffic light, the garbage would have slid forward, not backward onto the road, as he claims.

53 Slylock will return the painting on the left, which correctly shows the continents. Koppy Kat's forgery, on the right, has Africa and South America incorrectly placed.

54 Slylock knows that ice floats. Since the "ice" in the drinking glass is resting on the bottom, Slylock concludes that it is fake (probably made of glass) and was left by Count Weirdly to mislead them.

55 The car was stolen six months ago, during the bitter cold winter. Slylock suspects the thief drove the car on ice when the lake was frozen over.

56 Slylock Fox observed a burning lamp in the tomb.

57 An air current flows in the tunnel leading to the surface. If a match flame is held in its entrance, it will flicker from the current. The air in the dead-end tunnel is still.

58 There are no eggshells on or in the area around Slick Smitty. Slylock suspects Smitty broke the eggs himself to fake the robbery, and threw the shells in the trash, along with the bag of money.

59 Slylock Fox noticed that Count Weirdly's pen has its cap on. If Count Weirdly was suddenly attacked while writing with the pen, the cap would be off.

60 Slylock Fox knows that trees grow from the top. The tree trunk grows wider, but the nail would remain the same distance from the ground.

61 Slylock Fox can ask the bears to open their bottle. The root beer that was carried by the running shoplifter will overflow with a bubbly force when opened.

62 The sun's position is low in the sky and behind Slylock Fox. The escaped prisoner's long shadow crept in front of Slylock and alerted him.

63 Slylock Fox noted that both gloves at the scene are right-hand gloves. Slylock believes two thieves may have fled the scene wearing one glove, while leaving the right-hand gloves behind.

64 Slylock Fox knows that only female mosquitos suck blood. Since Mike the Monster Mosquito is male, he will only be feasting on flower nectar and plant juices.

65 Slylock Fox saw that the clock on the wall is battery powered and had stopped. (Notice the correct time on the outside clock.) Then he observed the loose battery on the small table. These clues led Slylock to suspect the tiny, stolen vial of diamonds are hidden in the clock's battery chamber.

66 The error in Koppy Kat's forged painting is the frog. Slylock Fox knows that frogs are freshwater creatures and do not inhabit the sea.

67 Slylock Fox strongly believes the tire track is not from a bike. He suspects both tracks were left by one thief pushing a wheelbarrow full of stolen tools.

68 Slylock Fox noticed that Shady Shrew has a wind-up alarm clock. It doesn't use electricity.

69 Count Weirdly's creepy tree creature will have a difficult time hiding among the normal maple trees because it will be the only tree in the winter forest that has leaves on its limbs.

70 It may be true that Reeky Rat and his bandmates did not carry vegetables *away* from Rachel Rabbit's garden, but Slylock Fox says it also may be true that they ate the vegetables while *in* the garden, making them responsible for the missing vegetables.

71 Slylock Fox suggested that sand be poured very slowly into the hole. Chester will be able to move his feet to stay on top of the sand as it slowly fills the hole. Eventually the sand will raise the chick high enough in the hole for Slylock to reach.

72 Slylock noticed that the white envelope is completely clean. If the chimney sweep's soot-covered hands had touched the envelope, he would have left marks.

73 Max observed and noted the car's license plate exactly as he saw it in the side mirror, which reversed the image of the plate. It actually reads 8HMO.

74 Slylock Fox noticed the pile of dirt on the other side of the courtyard fence, indicating that someone outside the fence dug the hole.

75 Count Weirdly is right-handed. (Notice the pencil in his right hand.) He would probably use his right hand to hold a hammer, yet it is his right hand that is bandaged.

76 Slylock Fox noticed a light bulb next to the trash basket. He believes Harry Ape replaced the bulb with the huge pearl.

77 The thief has established a pattern of stealing one part of items that come in pairs. Max's skateboard is not part of a pair.

78 When Slylock Fox was on the phone call he heard the sound of the crashing plate through the phone. The rat made the call, and he is the robber that plans to strike at 5:00 p.m.

79 Slylock Fox used his sense of taste to discover that the water dripping from the Super-Duper Jet Ski is freshwater, not salty ocean water. Confronted with the evidence, Count Weirdly admitted that he was the splasher.

80 Slick Smitty is wearing a watch that shows New York time, not Hawaii time, or even local Los Angeles time.

81 Slylock Fox attached the rabbit's bubble gum to the end of the goat's cane. Then he poked the sticky-tipped cane down through the jetty crevice onto the ring and lifted it up.

82 If Shady and his buddy shared a whole pizza equally, then there would not be an odd number of slices remaining. One is an odd number.

83 The dolphin is the surveillance robot. Count Weirdly mistakenly designed it with gills. Dolphins are air-breathing mammals; they do not have gills.

84 Slylock used the beam that gave way as a lever. He balanced it on top of a nearby rock, which acted as a fulcrum. Then he wedged one end of the beam under the boulder and pushed down on the other end. The boulder rolled slightly, and Max pulled out the map.

85 The broken shoestring dangling from the car door matches the raccoon's broken sneaker string. When confronted with the evidence, the raccoon confessed to stealing the car.

86 Slylock Fox touched the earrings and discovered they are very cold. They would have been room temperature if she had been in the dance club all evening. The wallet is in Cassandra's purse.

87 Slylock Fox found Rachel Rabbit's gold necklace underwater, attached to the hook on Buford Bear's fishing line.

88 The opposite of less is more. The rearranged letters spell the city of Rome.

89 Slylock Fox suggests they place blocks of ice on the pedestal between the ropes. Then, after lowering the sculpture onto the ice, the ropes could be cut loose. As the ice melts, the sculpture will gently settle onto the base.

90 Slylock Fox noticed the normal walking footprints and no crutch prints in the snow behind Cassandra Cat. She only pretended to use crutches when Slylock confronted her.

91 Harry Ape said, "I didn't walk past those shops." That's true, as the lie detector indicated. He went *into* each shop.

92 Because of Max Mouse's small size, his walking paces are much shorter than Slick Smitty's. Slylock Fox came to the scene, duplicated Smitty's long-legged stride, and successfully located the buried silver coins.

93 The bright lights of Las Vegas produce light pollution that obscures and diminishes the brilliance of the stars and planets, making this geographic location a poor site for viewing.

94 Slylock Fox could put the $50 bill inside a snowball and toss it across the ravine to Rachel Rabbit.

95 All of the windows and doors on Shady Shrew's car are closed. If Shady had escaped as it sank, there would probably still be an open door or window.

96 Shady Shrew's prize-winning fish is smaller than the other fish, but weighs ten pounds more. Slylock Fox suspects Shady stole the solid gold coins from Sir Hound's safe last night and hid them in the fish.

97 Slylock Fox suspects that Count Weirdly has not really been eating beef broth for the past 15 minutes because he is holding a fork, rather than a spoon.

98 If Max Mouse throws the ball straight up into the air, it will fall back into Max's hand.

99 The intruder stepped between Slylock and the tiny point of red light on the DVD player. When Slylock's view of the red light was blocked, he knew the intruder was in front of him, and that's when the fox grabbed him.

100 Slylock Fox pulled a spare tire out of his car trunk and tossed it to the fisherman. Spare tires float. After the man was rescued, Slylock strongly advised him to always put on a life jacket before getting into his boat.

101 The lighthouse shadow in the painting is wrongly cast toward the sun.

102 Slylock Fox is convinced the raccoon is lying. If he bought an ice cream cone 30 or more minutes ago, the ice cream would have melted in the heat.

103 Slylock Fox noticed that the spelling of Ms. Rabbit's first name, "Rachel," on her office door is different from the spelling of her name on the mean letters. Slylock doesn't think she would misspell her own name.

104 Slylock Fox noticed steam rising from Count Weirdly's bathwater. If the count had been asleep in the tub for the last hour, the water would not be steaming hot.

105 The prints that Slylock Fox found around the area of Grandpa Goat's gift basket are not fingerprints, they are toe prints. Like fingerprints, toe prints are unique to every human individual.

106 If the guard was blindfolded during the theft, he would not have known the robber's truck was green.

107 Slylock Fox observed Slick Smitty's clean-shaven face. If Smitty had been marooned on the island for five days he would probably have some noticeable facial stubble. Slylock suspects Slick Smitty is the chess set thief and had an accomplice bring him to the island to create his alibi.

108 When Roger Raccoon dropped Mrs. Beaver's gold wedding ring, one of the birds picked it up and swallowed it. Notice the round lump in its neck. Slylock helped the bird cough it up and returned it to Mrs. Beaver.

109 The spy device is transmitting all black images and muffled sound because as Slylock discovered, Count Weirdly's snake swallowed it. (Notice the round bulge.)

110 Neither Slylock Fox nor Max Mouse mentioned how much money was stolen from the bank. Yet Harry knew the exact amount of cash in the sacks.

111 The only way Cassandra Cat could have come ten miles from the mall in fifteen minutes is if she were driving an average of forty miles per hour. Since the posted speed limit for her journey is only twenty miles per hour, she definitely was speeding.

112 The restaurant chef and his assistant's vision was obscured. Their eyeglasses were fogged over because they entered the warm, humid kitchen from the cold refrigerator.

113 Slylock Fox knows that adult moths do not eat wool. It is only when they are in the larval (caterpillar) stage that they feed on wool and other fabrics. Count Weirdly is there to witness the reaction to his unkind prank, and Slylock is there to make sure the count is punished.

114 Reeky Rat said he will do 1,000 push-ups for ten dollars, but did not say he would do them all at the same time. The tricky rat could do some now and the rest at multiple other times, until the number totals 1,000.

115 Slylock Fox can take the painter's bucket and splash black paint over the robot's eyes to eliminate Count Weirdly's ability to guide the metal monster.

116 An owl cannot shift its eyes from side to side. An owl must turn its head to look to a side, as a world renowned nature artist would surely know. The painting with Koppy Kat's shifting eye error is the copy, and the other one is the original.

COLLECT
ALL THE BOOKS
IN THE GO FUN!
SERIES

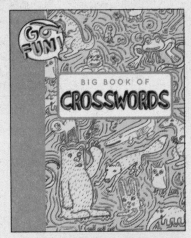